The Brown Donkey Goes To The Races

Margaret Molloy

Copyright ©2024 — Margaret Molloy —All Rights Reserved.

About The Author

Margaret Molloy is the author of *Agnes Morrogh- Bernard: Foundress of Foxford Woollen Mills* published in 2014 and *Martin Sheridan: Mayo's Famous Son 1881-1918* (2018). She is the co-author with Professor Peter Reid, Robert Gordon University, Aberdeen of Church and State: Censorship and Political Interference in the Libraries of County Mayo in *The Journal of Library and Information History* in May 2013 [Online] at www.tandfonline.com. Her work is mainly historical, with a special interest in local history. However, she has written a three children's books *The Brown Donkey,* (2020) published by Pegasus. *The Fairies Who Lost Their Powers* (2022) *published* by Austin Macauley *Climate Change* (2023) published by Pegasus. She has also written for *Ireland's Own, Ireland's Eye, The Irish Catholic, The Western People, The Mayo News and The Connaught Telegraph.*

Margaret holds a B A in English and History, and an MSc in Library and Information Studies. She lives in Bohola, in Co. Mayo.

Tim is so excited.

He has a huge smile on his face

His eyes are sparkling like the stars

Today is the big race

All the weeks of practice

That Fay and Don have done

The jumping, running, and the spins

Will commence with the starting gun

His brown hair is all shiny,

Tied up with sparkly bows.

With his lovely silver saddle,

He's a handsome donkey- he knows

Fay jumps lightly on his back

And takes the silver reins.

She whispers softly in his ear,

"We're faster than buses, trains, and planes."

They whizzed by all the donkeys,

Like a spinning top.

Tim's legs moved like lightning;

They couldn't seem to stop.

They whizzed by all the donkeys,

Like a spinning top.

Tim's legs moved like lightning;

They couldn't seem to stop.

Half-way down the track,

Tim let out a roar.

A big fat hippopotamus

Was pushing a lawn mower.

The other donkeys ran amok

And scattered in all directions.

Tim thought, "Now, I'll have to fly,

if there are no objections."

Tim flew high up in the sky

The hippo was no threat.

He landed down again from space

On land again- no sweat.

The other donkeys just looked on;

They couldn't believe their eyes

That Tim and Fay had won the race

And had got their special prize

Tim was so delighted.

He took off at such a pace;

He couldn't stop himself in time

And crashed into a heap of cakes.

His face was nowhere to be seen

Beneath a mix of jam and cream.

But as he began to lick his face,

You could see his brown eyes gleam.

Fay and Don, they washed his face

From all the jam and cream

And then discovered that his feet

Were stuck down in the stream

"Oh, dear, oh dear," cried Fay and Don,

"What are we to do?"

"Don't worry," said another voice,

"We will be helping you."

My name is Daphne donkey.

My husband Herb and sons Ron and Lou

We have a rope that's good and strong,

And we'll rescue Tim for you

And then, in the shortest time,

They tied the rope around Tim's tummy;

They hauled him out as good as new

And he cried, "Cakes, oh yummy."

"What a day, oh Fay and Don,

I've never been so happy.

Who says dreams don't come true?

So don't waste time just make it snappy."

www.ingramcontent.com/pod-product-compliance
Lightning Source LLC
LaVergne TN
LVHW081548060526
838200LV00048B/2259